A Brief History of Oman

KJ Smith

Copyright © 2025 KJ Smith

All rights reserved.

ISBN: 9798311889278

To the people of Oman, whose enduring spirit, rich traditions, and deep-rooted sense of identity continue to inspire and shape the future of this remarkable land.

Contents

INTRODUCTION 1
ANCIENT BEGINNINGS 4
RISE OF ANCIENT KINGDOMS 9
SPREAD OF ISLAM 15
OMAN UNDER THE IMAMS 21
RISE OF THE AL BU SA'ID DYNASTY 27
OMAN AND BRITISH INFLUENCE 34
REIGN OF SULTAN QABOOS BIN SAID 41
CONCLUSION 48
APPENDIX 53
ABOUT THE AUTHOR 59

INTRODUCTION

Oman, a country often overlooked in the annals of Middle Eastern history, is a land whose narrative is rich, diverse, and intricately woven into the fabric of global civilization. Positioned on the southeastern corner of the Arabian Peninsula, Oman holds a strategic geographic location that has been a crossroads of trade, culture, and religious development for millennia. Its rugged mountains, sprawling deserts, and pristine coastlines have been home to ancient peoples who contributed significantly to the development of the wider region. Yet despite its historical prominence, Oman remains somewhat of a mystery to many outside its borders.

This book aims to provide a concise yet comprehensive overview of Oman's history, from its earliest days to its present-day standing as a modern and progressive nation. The story of Oman is not just a narrative of political change, but one that reflects the persistence of a unique cultural identity shaped by its geography, its people, and its history. As one of the oldest independent states in the Arab world, Oman has maintained a sovereignty that is a testament to its resilience and determination in the face of external pressures.

In examining Oman's history, it is crucial to understand the interplay between its local traditions and the broader forces of history that have shaped the region. From ancient maritime trading networks to the rise of Islam, from the influence of colonial powers to its position as a neutral force in modern geopolitics, Oman has continuously adapted while preserving its cultural heritage. The Ibadhi sect of Islam, which has flourished in Oman, is a defining feature of its religious landscape, further contributing to its distinctiveness within the Islamic world.

Oman's history is also intrinsically tied to the sea. The Omani people have long been seafarers, traders, and explorers, navigating the Indian Ocean and establishing links with East Africa, India, and Southeast Asia. The maritime prowess of Oman played a crucial role in its expansion, establishing an empire that once stretched across the coasts of Zanzibar and beyond. This legacy of naval strength continues to shape Oman's identity today, from its modern navy to its proud traditions of seafaring.

At the heart of Oman's modern history is the reign of Sultan Qaboos bin Said, who ascended to the throne in 1970. Sultan Qaboos is credited with transforming Oman from a largely isolated and underdeveloped country into a prosperous nation with a stable political system, a growing economy, and a significant role in regional diplomacy. Under his leadership, Oman embraced a path of modernization while remaining deeply committed to its traditions. Sultan Qaboos's vision of a neutral and balanced foreign policy allowed Oman to maintain strong ties with both regional powers and the wider international community.

This book explores Oman's past through a variety of lenses—political, cultural, and economic—while paying homage to the country's unique contributions to the world. In the following chapters, we will delve into the ancient civilizations that flourished on Omani soil, the rise of Islam and its profound influence on Omani society, the maritime empire that once ruled the seas, and the nation-building efforts that shaped modern Oman. We will also examine the challenges Oman faces today as it continues to evolve in an increasingly complex and interconnected world.

As we journey through this brief history, we will come to appreciate the deep sense of pride and resilience that defines the Omani people. It is a history of endurance, of navigating the currents of time with wisdom, humility, and an unwavering commitment to preserving the essence of Oman's cultural and spiritual heritage.

This is the story of Oman—a land whose past is as captivating as its future is promising.

ANCIENT BEGINNINGS

The history of Oman stretches back far beyond the establishment of its modern borders, weaving a narrative that is as ancient as civilization itself. Oman's early history is a reflection of the country's strategic location at the crossroads of Africa, Asia, and the Arabian Peninsula. The land's rugged mountains, vast deserts, and fertile coastal plains have provided both a home and a resource-rich environment for its inhabitants, fostering the rise of some of the earliest known civilizations in the Middle East.

Prehistoric Oman: The Dawn of Civilization

Evidence of human settlement in Oman dates back to the Paleolithic era, with early traces of human life found in the Hajar Mountains and along the coastline. Archaeological findings, such as stone tools, ancient cave paintings, and remnants of early shelters, suggest that Oman's inhabitants were among the first in the Arabian Peninsula to develop a sophisticated way of life.

By the Neolithic period (around 5,000 BCE), the people of

A BRIEF HISTORY OF OMAN

Oman had begun to establish permanent settlements and engage in agriculture. The fertile valleys and plains of Oman, especially those in the interior, provided ample resources for the development of early communities. These early Omani societies were part of a broader network of trade and cultural exchange, linked to civilizations in Mesopotamia, Persia, and the Indus Valley. Oman's geographic location made it a vital conduit for trade routes that connected the distant corners of the ancient world, particularly the incense trade, which would become one of the defining features of Omani culture for centuries.

The Incense Trade and the Dilmun Civilization

Oman's role in the incense trade is perhaps one of its earliest and most significant contributions to world history. The people of ancient Oman were known for cultivating frankincense and myrrh, two highly prized substances that were used for religious rituals, medicine, and perfumes. These aromatic resins were transported by sea to the Mediterranean, the Arabian Peninsula, and beyond. The trade in incense and other luxury goods formed the foundation of Oman's early prosperity.

During the second millennium BCE, Oman was part of the thriving Dilmun civilization, a major trading power in the Arabian Gulf. Dilmun was not confined to present-day Oman, but it is believed that the heart of the civilization lay along Oman's coast, especially in the area around modern-day Sur. The Dilmun people were known for their advanced maritime skills, and their trade networks stretched from Mesopotamia and the Indus Valley to the Arabian Peninsula and the Arabian Gulf.

The Dilmun civilization flourished as a center of commerce,

and archaeological evidence suggests that it played a key role in the exchange of goods, ideas, and cultural practices between different regions. Dilmun was an essential node in the trade networks of the ancient world, facilitating not only the movement of incense but also metals, textiles, and agricultural products. The region's strategic importance made it a crucial part of the wider dynamics of ancient trade and diplomacy.

The Influence of Ancient Powers: From the Sumerians to the Persians

The ancient history of Oman is also marked by the influence of neighboring powers, such as the Sumerians, Akkadians, and later the Persians. The Sumerians of Mesopotamia, who were among the first to establish written records, referred to Oman as "Magan," a rich land famed for its resources, particularly copper. Oman's copper mines, especially in the region of Sohar, became a source of great economic significance and played a pivotal role in the ancient world's metallurgy.

The Persian influence over Oman began to grow in the first millennium BCE as the Achaemenid Empire expanded its borders. Oman became a part of the Persian satrapy of Oman and maintained close ties with the Persian Empire. This period saw the integration of Omani society into the broader Persian sphere, which brought with it advancements in trade, culture, and military techniques.

The influence of the Persian Empire was followed by the rise of the Sassanid Empire, which continued to assert control over Oman in the centuries leading up to the rise of Islam. During this period, Oman's coastal cities became vital ports for the trade of goods between Persia and the Indian Ocean world. The Sassanids left their mark on Omani architecture, religion, and social structures, paving the way for the eventual spread of Islam in the region.

The Ancient Kingdoms and Early Omani Culture

By the time Islam arrived in Oman in the 7th century CE, the region had already developed a distinct cultural and religious identity. The coastal cities and towns of Oman were known for their unique blend of Arabian and Persian influences, which shaped the region's early cultural development. The Omani people's long history of trade, interaction with neighboring empires, and reliance on the sea for sustenance created a cosmopolitan culture that was both open to external influences and fiercely protective of its traditions.

As Oman moved from the ancient world into the early medieval period, its cities, ports, and people played a key role in the broader history of the Arabian Peninsula. The ancient foundations of Omani society—rooted in its maritime prowess, its role as a trade hub, and its connections to distant civilizations—would continue to shape the country for centuries to come.

Conclusion

The ancient beginnings of Oman are marked by its contributions to trade, culture, and religious development, laying the groundwork for the complex and multifaceted society that would emerge in later centuries. The strategic importance of Oman's geographic location, its rich natural resources, and its cultural openness to foreign influences helped shape the course of its early history. From the rise of the Dilmun civilization to the influence of the Persians, Oman's ancient roots set the stage for its eventual role as a center of Islamic culture, a maritime power, and a nation with a deep sense of independence and identity.

As we continue to explore the history of Oman, it becomes evident that the country's ancient past is not simply a series of isolated events but a continuous thread of cultural, political, and economic development that has shaped its modern identity and its place in the world.

A BRIEF HISTORY OF OMAN

RISE OF ANCIENT KINGDOMS

The ancient history of Oman is characterized by the emergence of several powerful and influential kingdoms, each contributing to the development of the region's social, political, and economic landscape. These kingdoms laid the foundations for Oman's distinctive identity, and their legacy can still be seen today in the country's rich cultural heritage, trade traditions, and strategic positioning in the Gulf.

The Kingdom of Dilmun: The Heart of Trade

One of the earliest and most significant civilizations in Oman was the kingdom of Dilmun. The Dilmun civilization flourished from around 3,000 BCE to 1,000 BCE, and its reach extended far beyond the boundaries of modern Oman, encompassing parts of Bahrain, Eastern Saudi Arabia, and Kuwait. While the exact extent of Dilmun's territory is debated, archaeological evidence suggests that its heart lay along Oman's eastern coastline, particularly in the area around the city of Sur.

A BRIEF HISTORY OF OMAN

Dilmun's prominence as a trade hub can be attributed to its strategic location at the crossroads of ancient maritime trade routes. The people of Dilmun were known for their advanced maritime skills, which enabled them to establish a vast network of trade connections with Mesopotamia, the Indus Valley, and the Arabian Peninsula. Their ships carried valuable goods such as frankincense, myrrh, and copper, which were highly prized by other civilizations in the ancient world.

Dilmun's importance as a trade center made it one of the wealthiest and most influential kingdoms of its time. The trade in incense, in particular, played a key role in the kingdom's prosperity. Incense was used in religious ceremonies, perfumes, and medicines, and its value made it a highly sought-after commodity across the ancient world. The people of Dilmun were skilled in the production and trade of this valuable resin, which came from trees that grew in the mountains of Oman.

Archaeological excavations have revealed the remains of Dilmun's extensive trading infrastructure, including ports, warehouses, and temples. These sites, particularly the ancient city of Qalhat (near modern Sur), provide important insights into the kingdom's role in connecting the ancient world's major cultures. The Dilmunites not only engaged in trade but also played a role in the cultural exchange between Mesopotamia, the Indus Valley, and the Arabian Peninsula. Through this exchange, they adopted and adapted various artistic, religious, and technological innovations, which would later influence the development of Oman's own culture.

The Himyarite Kingdom: Oman's Link to South Arabia

A BRIEF HISTORY OF OMAN

As Dilmun declined, the Himyarite Kingdom rose to prominence in the south of the Arabian Peninsula, in what is now Yemen. The Himyarites controlled much of the southern Arabian Peninsula, including parts of modern-day Oman. Their rise to power marked a new era in Omani history, as the kingdom of Himyar had a profound influence on Oman's culture, religion, and economy.

The Himyarites were known for their advanced agricultural techniques, which allowed them to thrive in the arid deserts of southern Arabia. They established extensive trade routes that connected Oman to the rest of the Arabian Peninsula, Africa, and India. The Himyarites were also known for their religious and cultural contributions, including their role in the spread of the South Arabian script, which would later influence the development of Arabic script.

The Himyarite Kingdom's influence in Oman was not just economic but also religious. The Himyarites practiced a form of polytheism, with their pantheon of gods including deities associated with the moon, sun, and stars. However, their most significant religious contribution to Oman was the introduction of Judaism. By the 5th century CE, many Himyarite rulers had adopted Judaism, and the religion spread into Oman, particularly among the coastal regions. This early presence of Judaism would later be eclipsed by the rise of Islam, but it played a key role in shaping Oman's religious diversity.

The Himyarites were also known for their military prowess, and they played a key role in defending Oman against external threats. As Oman's strategic location in the Arabian Gulf became more important, the Himyarites recognized the need to maintain control over the region's trade routes. However, their dominance was eventually challenged by the rise of other powers, including the Persian Empire, which would come to control Oman in the centuries that followed.

The Sassanid Empire: Persian Influence on Oman

By the 3rd century CE, the Persian Sassanid Empire had become the dominant power in the region, and its influence extended into Oman. The Sassanids, who ruled Persia from 224 CE to 651 CE, sought to control the trade routes that passed through Oman and the Arabian Gulf. Oman's strategic location made it a valuable prize for the Sassanid Empire, and the Persians established a presence in the region.

Under the Sassanids, Oman was integrated into the wider Persian sphere of influence. The Sassanids brought with them a number of cultural, religious, and technological advancements that would shape Omani society for centuries. The Persians introduced Zoroastrianism to Oman, which would coexist alongside the region's pre-existing polytheistic traditions. Persian influence can also be seen in Omani architecture, art, and military organization.

The Sassanids saw Oman as a vital part of their empire, both for its resources and its strategic location along the trade routes to India and Africa. Omani ports such as Sohar became important trading centers, linking the Persian Empire with the rest of the Indian Ocean world. Sohar, in particular, was known for its thriving trade in copper, which was mined in the mountains of Oman and traded with other civilizations.

A BRIEF HISTORY OF OMAN

The Sassanid Empire's influence on Oman was not without challenges. The local Omani population, especially in the interior regions, resisted Persian control and maintained a degree of independence. This resistance would eventually lead to the emergence of a new political and religious movement in Oman, one that would shape the country's future for centuries to come.

Oman's Path Toward Islam

By the 7th century CE, the stage was set for the arrival of a transformative force that would reshape Omani society: Islam. The rise of the Islamic caliphate in the Arabian Peninsula had profound implications for Oman, as it did for the rest of the region. Oman's early embrace of Islam and its subsequent role in the development of the Ibadhi sect would mark a new chapter in the country's history, one that would blend the influences of ancient kingdoms with the new religious and political order brought by the Arab conquest.

But before the arrival of Islam, Oman's ancient kingdoms had already established a legacy of trade, cultural exchange, and religious diversity that would help shape the country's unique identity within the Islamic world.

Conclusion

The rise of the ancient kingdoms in Oman—Dilmun, Himyar, and the Sassanid Empire—laid the groundwork for the country's development as a strategic and influential power in the region. These kingdoms brought with them advanced trade networks, cultural exchange, and religious influences that would shape Oman's future. From the incense trade to the spread of Judaism and Zoroastrianism, Oman's ancient history is a story of cultural adaptation and resilience. The legacy of these kingdoms continues to resonate in Oman's modern identity, as the country remains a crossroads of cultures and a vital player in the history of the Arabian Peninsula.

SPREAD OF ISLAM

The arrival of Islam in Oman in the 7th century marked a pivotal moment in the country's history, one that would forever shape its political, cultural, and religious identity. Like much of the Arabian Peninsula, Oman was to be transformed by the teachings of the Prophet Muhammad and the rapid expansion of the Islamic caliphate. However, Oman's response to Islam and the religious path it would follow diverged from many of its neighbors, leading to the establishment of the Ibadhi sect, which continues to be a defining feature of Omani society today.

The Early Years: Islam's Arrival in Oman

Islam arrived in Oman during the lifetime of the Prophet Muhammad, shortly after the initial revelation of Islam. The region had been home to various forms of polytheism and Jewish communities, and its people were no strangers to religious diversity. By the time Islam spread across the Arabian Peninsula in the early 7th century, Oman had already begun to feel the influence of Arab traders and Islamic emissaries.

A BRIEF HISTORY OF OMAN

The initial contacts with Islam were peaceful and led to conversions among various tribal leaders and groups within Oman. However, the conversion of Oman was not immediate or uniform. The first significant encounter between Omani leaders and the early Muslims occurred when a delegation from Oman visited Medina, the city where the Prophet Muhammad had established the nascent Islamic community. The delegation sought guidance and spiritual direction from the Prophet and his followers.

After this visit, the people of Oman largely embraced Islam, but there was significant debate about how best to organize their religious and political lives. While some Omani tribes accepted the leadership of the caliphs in Medina, others resisted the authority of the central caliphate, which led to internal divisions. This tension would eventually result in the establishment of a distinctive Omani interpretation of Islam: Ibadhi Islam.

The Rise of Ibadhi Islam

Ibadhi Islam, which took its name from Abdullah ibn Ibadh, was a moderate, reformist branch of Islam that emphasized a form of religious purity and political independence. The Ibadhi sect distinguished itself from both Sunni and Shia branches of Islam by advocating for a more egalitarian, non-hereditary form of leadership and by placing a strong emphasis on the principles of piety, justice, and communal welfare.

The formation of the Ibadhi sect was, in many ways, a response to the political and religious conflicts that characterized the early Islamic community. During the first centuries of Islam, the Muslim world was embroiled in civil wars and power struggles between different factions, notably the Sunni and Shia branches. In contrast to these sectarian conflicts, the Ibadhi movement promoted a form of Islam that sought to avoid political partisanship and factionalism. This appeal for neutrality and moderation resonated strongly with many Omanis, who sought a path that would allow them to maintain their independence from the larger caliphates of the time.

The Ibadhi movement became firmly established in Oman by the 8th century, when the first Ibadhi imams (religious leaders) were elected. The role of the imam in Ibadhi Islam was not hereditary, as in many other Islamic traditions, but was instead determined by the community's choice. This practice reinforced the Ibadhi commitment to a form of government based on consensus, consultation, and merit rather than inherited power. The election of the imam was often an inclusive process that involved the participation of the community, from the tribal leaders to the common people, reflecting the democratic and communal spirit of Ibadhi thought.

Over time, the influence of the Ibadhi sect in Oman grew, and it became the dominant religious and political force in the country. This laid the foundation for Oman's unique identity within the Islamic world, where it would remain largely independent from the larger caliphates in both the spiritual and political realms.

Oman's Role in the Islamic Caliphate

Despite its early embrace of Islam, Oman maintained a measure of independence from the central caliphates that emerged in the centuries following the death of the Prophet Muhammad. Initially, Oman was part of the Rashidun Caliphate (632–661), the first Islamic caliphate, but it became increasingly distant from the political control of the Umayyad and Abbasid caliphates that succeeded it.

Throughout the early centuries of Islam, Oman maintained its own imams, who exercised both religious and political authority. The imams were recognized as the legitimate leaders of the Omani people, and their authority was rooted in religious scholarship and the principles of Ibadhi Islam. These imams often found themselves in conflict with the central caliphates, particularly during the Umayyad and Abbasid periods, when the power of the caliphate was consolidated and centralized in Damascus and Baghdad, respectively.

Oman's independence from the caliphates was solidified during periods of resistance, most notably during the conflict with the Umayyads in the 8th century. Oman's refusal to accept Umayyad rule led to several uprisings, with the most famous being the Battle of the Camel in 746 CE. This rebellion was part of a broader resistance movement against the Umayyads, who sought to impose their authority over the region. Although the Umayyads were ultimately able to maintain their control over much of the Arabian Peninsula, Oman remained steadfast in its commitment to independence and the leadership of its Ibadhi imams.

The Golden Age of the Ibadhi Imams

The 9th and 10th centuries were considered a golden age for Ibadhi Islam in Oman. During this period, Oman enjoyed a relatively high degree of stability and prosperity, thanks in large part to its flourishing trade networks, strong agricultural base, and the influence of the Ibadhi imams. Oman's strategic location at the mouth of the Arabian Gulf allowed it to control important maritime trade routes, connecting the Arabian Peninsula with East Africa, India, and the wider Indian Ocean world.

The Ibadhi imams of this period were not just religious leaders; they also played a key role in governance and diplomacy. They were responsible for maintaining the social order, administering justice, and ensuring the welfare of their communities. In many ways, the imams were the embodiment of the ideal Ibadhi leadership: just, pious, and chosen by the people. The imams were also active in external diplomacy, maintaining relations with other Islamic states as well as neighboring non-Islamic powers, including the Persian Gulf states and East African kingdoms.

Under the leadership of the Ibadhi imams, Oman became a beacon of religious and political autonomy. The country's commitment to Ibadhi Islam, which emphasized both the spiritual and temporal aspects of leadership, allowed it to maintain a sense of unity and continuity, even as other parts of the Islamic world were torn apart by sectarian conflicts.

Oman's Isolation and Independence

As the centuries progressed, Oman continued to distance itself from the larger Islamic caliphates. This political isolation, coupled with the country's commitment to Ibadhi Islam, meant that Oman developed a unique identity that was distinct from its Sunni and Shia neighbors. Oman's imams continued to lead the country until the 20th century, when the arrival of foreign powers and the discovery of oil began to alter the country's political landscape.

Despite these changes, the religious and cultural legacy of Ibadhi Islam has endured in Oman, shaping the country's political institutions, social structure, and worldview. The commitment to consultation, community welfare, and religious purity that characterized the early years of Ibadhi Islam remains a central tenet of Omani society today.

Conclusion

The spread of Islam in Oman and the subsequent establishment of Ibadhi Islam played a defining role in shaping the country's religious, political, and cultural landscape. Oman's embrace of Islam was not only a spiritual transformation but also a political and social revolution that set it apart from other parts of the Arabian Peninsula. The rise of Ibadhi Islam created a distinctive Omani identity, one that has remained largely unchanged despite centuries of external influence and internal change. Today, Oman remains a unique bastion of Ibadhi thought and practice, a legacy of the country's long history of religious independence and resilience.

A BRIEF HISTORY OF OMAN

OMAN UNDER THE IMAMS

The rise of Ibadhi Islam and the establishment of the Ibadhi imamate marked a distinct phase in Oman's history, one in which religious and political leadership were intricately intertwined. Unlike many other regions of the Islamic world, Oman maintained a unique system of governance, where religious leaders, or imams, exercised both spiritual and temporal authority. This political model, rooted in the principles of Ibadhi Islam, provided Oman with a sense of independence, stability, and continuity for centuries.

The Imamate System: A Distinct Political Tradition

The foundation of Oman's political system during this period lay in the imamate, a religious and political institution unique to Oman. Unlike the hereditary caliphates that dominated much of the Islamic world, the imamate was a system of elected leadership, where the imam was chosen by the community, often through a process of consultation and consensus. The imam, once chosen, had a dual role: he was both a religious scholar, guiding the people in spiritual matters, and a political leader, governing the state in accordance with Islamic principles.

The role of the imam was not just to lead the prayers and provide spiritual guidance, but also to ensure justice, peace, and the welfare of the people. Imams were responsible for the administration of justice, the collection of taxes, and the defense of the state. They also had the authority to oversee the implementation of Sharia law, although the Ibadhi interpretation of Sharia emphasized consultation (shura) and consensus (ijma) over strict legalism. This led to a governance system that valued the opinions of the community and sought to avoid arbitrary rule.

The political and spiritual role of the imam was balanced by the participation of local councils and tribal leaders in decision-making. This made the system of governance more democratic compared to the centralization seen in other Islamic states. The Omani imamate was grounded in the belief that political authority should be earned through piety, wisdom, and consensus, rather than inherited or imposed by force.

The Imams and the Struggle for Independence

Oman's early imams faced numerous challenges, particularly from foreign powers seeking to assert control over the region. One of the most notable periods of external pressure occurred during the expansion of the Umayyad and Abbasid Caliphates. While many regions of the Arabian Peninsula accepted the authority of the central caliphates, Oman's imams resisted such control, maintaining a sense of autonomy and self-governance. This resistance to outside authority would become a hallmark of Omani history.

The struggle for independence reached its peak in the 8th century during the conflict with the Umayyads. The Umayyad caliphate, based in Damascus, sought to bring Oman under its control, but the Omani people, under the leadership of their imams, rebelled against this foreign influence. The resistance culminated in the Battle of the Camel in 746 CE, a pivotal moment in Omani history. The defeat of the Umayyad forces signaled that Oman would remain independent from the central authority of the caliphate, and the Ibadhi imams would continue to govern without external interference.

This resistance to foreign rule continued through the Abbasid period, as Oman maintained its independence despite the growing power of the Abbasid caliphate in Baghdad. While the Abbasids were able to exert some influence over Oman, particularly in the early years, the imams and the Omani people remained largely autonomous, preserving their unique political and religious system.

The Golden Age of the Imams

The period from the 9th to the 13th centuries is often considered the golden age of the Omani imamate. During this time, Oman experienced political stability, economic prosperity, and religious unity under the leadership of its imams. The Ibadhi imams oversaw the growth of a prosperous maritime economy, with Oman becoming a major trading hub connecting the Arabian Peninsula with East Africa, India, and beyond.

The imams also played a central role in fostering a sense of national unity. They were not only spiritual leaders but also symbolic figures of Omani identity and resistance to foreign domination. The imamate was closely linked to Oman's distinctive culture, its adherence to Ibadhi principles, and its commitment to maintaining independence from the larger Islamic world.

Economically, Oman flourished during this period due to its strategic position along the maritime trade routes. The ports of Sohar, Muscat, and Sur became key centers of commerce, facilitating trade in goods such as frankincense, myrrh, copper, and textiles. Oman's maritime traders and sailors were known throughout the Indian Ocean world, and the country became a key player in the global economy.

Culturally, the period was marked by intellectual growth. Omani scholars, particularly those from the Ibadhi tradition, contributed to the development of Islamic theology, jurisprudence, and philosophy. The imams encouraged learning and the pursuit of knowledge, and Oman became home to a vibrant intellectual community that sought to reconcile Islamic teachings with the practical realities of governance and daily life.

Decline and Challenges to the Imamate

Despite the successes of the Ibadhi imamate, the political and religious system began to face challenges by the 14th century. Internal divisions, external invasions, and the growing influence of regional powers gradually eroded the strength of the imamate.

One of the key challenges was the rise of powerful external forces, such as the Portuguese and later the Persian Safavids, who sought to exert control over Oman's key ports and trade routes.

A BRIEF HISTORY OF OMAN

The Portuguese, in particular, established a strong presence in Oman during the early 16th century, capturing the strategic city of Muscat and using it as a base for their operations in the Indian Ocean. This foreign occupation undermined the authority of the imams and led to a period of turmoil and resistance.

In addition to foreign intervention, internal conflicts within Oman's tribes and factions weakened the unity of the imamate. By the late 17th century, the imams' authority was challenged by the rise of powerful tribal leaders and the fragmentation of Omani society. These challenges were compounded by the growing influence of external powers in the region, which continued to challenge Oman's independence.

The Revival of the Imamate: The Al Ya'rubi Dynasty

Despite these challenges, the concept of the imamate was revived in the 17th century under the leadership of the Al Ya'rubi dynasty. This period marked a resurgence of Omani power and independence, as the Al Ya'rubi family, in alliance with the imams, led Oman to victory against Portuguese forces. The recapture of Muscat in 1650 was a turning point in Omani history, signaling the restoration of the imamate system and the reassertion of Omani independence.

The Al Ya'rubi period is also notable for the expansion of Omani influence, as Oman became a major naval power in the Indian Ocean. The revival of the imamate under the Al Ya'rubi dynasty marked the return of Oman to its roots as an independent Islamic state, committed to the principles of Ibadhi Islam and self-governance.

A BRIEF HISTORY OF OMAN

The Imamate's Decline and Transition to Sultanate Rule

By the 18th century, however, the imamate system began to decline once again, as external pressures and internal divisions continued to mount. The rise of the Al Bu Sa'id family in the mid-18th century marked the transition from an imamate-based system of government to the Sultanate of Oman, which would later become the modern state of Oman.

The transition from the imamate to the Sultanate was a gradual process, and it did not erase the significance of the imamate in Omani society. Even after the Sultanate was established, the role of the imam remained an important part of Oman's identity, influencing the political landscape and contributing to the sense of national unity.

Conclusion

The period of the imamate in Oman represents a distinctive chapter in the country's history, one characterized by a unique system of governance that blended religious leadership with political authority. The imams of Oman were not only spiritual guides but also the defenders of the country's independence, guiding the people through centuries of external challenges and internal struggles. The imamate system allowed Oman to develop a strong sense of identity and autonomy that set it apart from the rest of the Islamic world. While the imamate eventually gave way to the Sultanate, the legacy of the imams continues to resonate in Oman's political and religious life to this day.

A BRIEF HISTORY OF OMAN

RISE OF THE AL BU SA'ID DYNASTY

The transition from the Imamate system to the Sultanate of Oman marks one of the most significant shifts in the country's history. The 18th century saw Oman's internal and external struggles come to a head, with the decline of the imamate and the eventual rise of the Al Bu Sa'id dynasty. This chapter delves into the factors that led to this change, the role of the Al Bu Sa'id family, and the early steps towards modernization and consolidation of Omani power.

The Decline of the Imamate and Internal Strife

By the early 18th century, Oman was embroiled in internal strife, economic challenges, and external threats, all of which contributed to the weakening of the imamate system. The internal divisions between different tribes, factions, and regions within Oman had long been a source of instability, and by the late 17th century, the unity that the imamate had once provided began to crumble.

A BRIEF HISTORY OF OMAN

The decline of the imamate coincided with growing European intervention in the Indian Ocean and Persian Gulf, particularly by the Portuguese and later the British. The Portuguese had established a significant presence in Oman during the 16th century, occupying key ports like Muscat and controlling trade routes. Although the Portuguese were expelled in the mid-17th century by Omani forces under the leadership of the Al Ya'rubi family, the struggle for control of Oman's ports and trade routes did not end.

Despite the victory over the Portuguese, Oman's internal struggles persisted, and its political system became increasingly fragmented. The imamate's leadership faced competition from powerful local tribal leaders who sought more power, and the weakening central authority left Oman vulnerable to both internal uprisings and external invasions.

The Rise of the Al Bu Sa'id Family

In the midst of this turmoil, the Al Bu Sa'id family emerged as a key political force in Oman. The family traces its origins to the early 18th century, with the rise of Ahmed bin Said, a tribal leader who played a central role in unifying Oman in the face of foreign threats. In 1744, Ahmed bin Said was chosen as the imam of Oman, marking the beginning of the Al Bu Sa'id dynasty. His ascension to power came at a crucial moment, as Oman faced the combined threat of internal disintegration and continued foreign interference.

The Al Bu Sa'id family quickly consolidated power by forging alliances with various tribal leaders and military forces. One of the most significant events during this period was the expulsion of the Persian Safavids, who had briefly occupied parts of Oman in the early 18th century. The Al Bu Sa'id family, with the support of local tribes, successfully ousted the Safavids and restored Omani control over its territories.

However, the rise of the Al Bu Sa'id family was not without controversy. The imamate system, which had long been the foundation of Omani governance, was increasingly challenged by the Al Bu Sa'id family's leadership. The shift from the elected imamate to a dynastic rule marked a significant transformation in Omani politics, signaling the end of the traditional system of governance based on religious and tribal consensus.

Despite this shift, the Al Bu Sa'id family maintained the outward trappings of the imamate system. While the imam continued to be an important figure, especially in religious matters, the Sultan became the de facto ruler, taking on the responsibilities of governing and military leadership. The political structure in Oman gradually shifted towards a more centralized, monarchical system.

Consolidation of Power and the Role of the Al Bu Sa'id Sultanate

Under the leadership of the Al Bu Sa'id family, Oman began to consolidate its power and rebuild its political and economic structures. The new dynasty focused on strengthening the country's military, securing its borders, and expanding its influence in the region. The leadership of the Al Bu Sa'id family was instrumental in restoring Oman's sovereignty and bringing stability to a country that had long been racked by internal divisions and foreign invasions.

A BRIEF HISTORY OF OMAN

One of the key accomplishments of the Al Bu Sa'id dynasty during this period was the re-establishment of Oman's maritime empire. Oman had long been a significant naval power in the Indian Ocean, and under the Al Bu Sa'id family, the country's navy was strengthened, allowing Oman to dominate trade routes and assert its influence over coastal areas in East Africa, the Persian Gulf, and the Indian subcontinent.

In addition to military and territorial expansion, the Al Bu Sa'id family also worked to stabilize Oman's internal political situation. They sought to balance the power of local tribal leaders while maintaining control over key regions, such as Muscat and the interior. The Al Bu Sa'id sultans worked to integrate Oman's tribal and religious factions into the broader political structure, ensuring their loyalty while also maintaining the legitimacy of the Sultanate.

Despite these efforts, the transition to a Sultanate system was not without its challenges. The country remained divided in many ways, with the interior regions still holding significant autonomy and maintaining their allegiance to the imamate. Tensions between the Sultanate and the imamate flared at various points during the 18th and 19th centuries, with the imams periodically asserting their authority over the Sultan.

Oman's Maritime Empire: The Height of Omani Influence

During the 18th and early 19th centuries, Oman reached the height of its influence as a maritime power. The country's strategic location along key trade routes allowed it to control much of the trade between the Arabian Peninsula, East Africa, and the Indian subcontinent. Omani merchants were heavily involved in the trade of valuable commodities such as frankincense, gold, ivory, and slaves, and Oman became a crucial player in the global economy.

The Omani navy, under the Al Bu Sa'id leadership, was one of the most powerful in the Indian Ocean. The sultans established a network of fortified ports along the coast of East Africa, including Zanzibar, and established their presence in the Persian Gulf, where they competed with the Portuguese and later the British for control of key maritime trade routes.

In East Africa, Oman exercised considerable influence over the Swahili Coast, with Zanzibar emerging as a key center of trade and culture. The Omani sultans established a semi-autonomous Sultanate in Zanzibar in the early 19th century, which became an important part of Oman's maritime empire.

However, Omani control over East Africa began to wane in the 19th century due to the growing influence of European colonial powers, particularly the British. The British, through their colonial presence in India and their naval dominance in the Indian Ocean, began to challenge Oman's hold on its overseas territories.

The Beginning of Modernization: Influence of the British

As Oman entered the 19th century, the country faced increasing pressure from European powers, particularly the British, who sought to exert their influence over the region's trade and politics. The British, in particular, had a strategic interest in Oman's ports, as they provided access to key maritime routes and served as a buffer against potential Russian expansion in the region.

The relationship between Oman and Britain evolved through the 19th century. Initially, the British maintained a relatively hands-off approach to Oman, respecting the country's independence and maintaining friendly relations with the sultans. However, as Britain expanded its influence in the Indian Ocean, it became increasingly involved in Omani affairs.

In 1798, the British signed a treaty with Oman that recognized Omani sovereignty over its territories while allowing Britain to protect its maritime interests in the region. Over time, this relationship deepened, with Oman increasingly aligning itself with British interests, particularly in terms of trade, defense, and foreign policy.

Despite the growing influence of Britain, the Al Bu Sa'id family continued to assert Oman's sovereignty and worked to maintain the country's independence. The Sultanate maintained its political and economic power, even as British influence in the region continued to grow.

Conclusion: A Transition to the Modern Era

The 18th and early 19th centuries were transformative years for Oman, as the country navigated internal divisions, external threats, and the shift from an imamate-based system of governance to the rise of the Al Bu Sa'id Sultanate. The Al Bu Sa'id family's leadership brought stability to Oman, allowing the country to rebuild its power and influence, particularly in the maritime realm.

A BRIEF HISTORY OF OMAN

While the Al Bu Sa'id dynasty faced challenges both internally and externally, its leadership laid the groundwork for Oman's eventual transition into the modern era. The combination of political consolidation, economic prosperity through trade, and a strong military presence allowed Oman to flourish despite the pressures of European colonialism. The legacy of the Al Bu Sa'id family continues to shape Oman's political structure and its approach to foreign relations, providing a foundation for the country's future growth and development.

A BRIEF HISTORY OF OMAN

OMAN AND BRITISH INFLUENCE

The 19th century was a period of profound transformation for Oman. Although the country had long resisted foreign domination, the growing influence of European powers in the Indian Ocean—particularly that of the British Empire—forced Oman to recalibrate its political and economic landscape. By the mid-1800s, Oman was no longer the independent maritime empire it once was; instead, it was drawn into the complex web of British interests in the region, marking the beginning of a new era of modernization, foreign diplomacy, and economic development.

Oman and the British Protectorate: The Treaty of 1798

At the turn of the 19th century, Oman's position on key maritime routes between the Arabian Peninsula, East Africa, and the Indian subcontinent made it a strategic location for any global power seeking to control trade in the region. With the rise of the British East India Company and the growing importance of British trade interests in the Indian Ocean, Oman found itself under increasing pressure from the British to align its policies with theirs.

The first significant step in this new relationship came with the signing of the Treaty of 1798 between the Sultan of Oman, Said bin Sultan, and the British government. This agreement was a turning point for Oman, as it formalized Britain's strategic interests in the region while maintaining Oman's sovereignty. In the treaty, Britain recognized Oman's control over its territories in the Arabian Peninsula, the Persian Gulf, and East Africa, while the Sultan agreed to allow Britain to protect Oman's trade routes from piracy and external threats.

This treaty set the stage for a period of increasing British involvement in Oman's affairs. While the British did not directly govern Oman, their influence in the region began to shape Omani foreign policy and military strategy. The British provided the Sultanate with military support, which was essential for maintaining control over Oman's overseas territories, including Zanzibar, a key hub of Omani power in East Africa.

The growing relationship with Britain also meant that Oman would increasingly be drawn into the wider colonial struggle for influence in the Middle East and Indian Ocean. While Oman's leaders maintained a degree of independence, they could no longer act solely on their own terms without considering British interests.

The Zanzibar Sultanate: Oman's African Dominion

The 19th century saw Oman's maritime empire at its peak, particularly through the Sultanate's control of Zanzibar. Located off the coast of East Africa, Zanzibar became a thriving port for trade and commerce, particularly in slaves, ivory, and spices. The island, which had been part of Oman's empire since the mid-17th century, was solidified as the center of Oman's African holdings by Sultan Said bin Sultan in the early 1800s.

Said bin Sultan's decision to establish his seat of government in Zanzibar, rather than Muscat, marked a significant shift in Omani priorities. Under his leadership, the island flourished as a key commercial and cultural center, with Omani merchants controlling a significant portion of the trade across the Indian Ocean. Zanzibar was a melting pot of cultures, with a population that included Arabs, Africans, Indians, and Europeans. The Sultanate's control over Zanzibar made Oman an influential force in East Africa, with Oman's navy patrolling the coast and protecting trade routes from pirates.

However, Zanzibar's wealth and strategic importance would also attract the attention of European powers, particularly the British. As Britain expanded its imperial ambitions in the region, the balance of power in Zanzibar and Oman began to shift. By the mid-19th century, British influence over Zanzibar was growing, especially with the signing of treaties that placed the island under British protectorate status in 1890. Although Oman nominally retained control over Zanzibar, it was now under the heavy shadow of British imperialism.

The decline of Omani power in Zanzibar was not just due to British pressure, but also internal divisions. The island's growing prominence brought about challenges to the Sultan's control from rival factions, which weakened Oman's ability to manage its distant territories effectively.

Internal Struggles: The Collapse of the Imamate and the Emergence of Sultanate Rule

The internal political landscape in Oman during the 19th century was characterized by a struggle for power between the Sultan and the imamate. As we saw in previous chapters, the imamate had once played a central role in Omani governance, but by the early 1800s, the rise of the Al Bu Sa'id dynasty had shifted the country toward a more centralized form of rule under the Sultan.

Despite the Sultan's increasing control, the influence of the imamate remained strong in the interior regions of Oman. The country's interior was still home to many tribes that held allegiance to the imams, and there were occasional uprisings against the Sultan's authority. The imams, who saw themselves as the legitimate leaders of Oman, resisted the Sultan's attempts to consolidate power.

The 19th century saw several revolts in the interior, most notably the revolt led by the Imam of Oman, Sayyid Muhammad bin Abd Allah, in the 1850s. These uprisings reflected a deep-seated resistance to the centralized rule of the Sultan and the growing influence of British interests. The interior of Oman remained a largely autonomous region, with imams continuing to lead the local population and often challenging the Sultan's authority.

Despite these challenges, the Sultan of Oman, aided by British support, gradually emerged victorious in these conflicts. The imamate system slowly faded into the background, and Sultan

Said bin Sultan's heirs, particularly Sultan Qaboos bin Said, became the undisputed leaders of Oman. The establishment of a Sultanate with consolidated power became the new political reality for Oman, although it was a shift that would require navigating the complex relationships between internal factions and external pressures, particularly from the British.

Economic Changes: The Growth of Trade and Infrastructure Development

In addition to political changes, the 19th century brought about important economic shifts in Oman. The growth of trade, particularly through the country's maritime routes, helped fuel the development of Oman's infrastructure. As Oman's strategic ports—such as Muscat, Sur, and Zanzibar—became key hubs of commerce, the country's economy became increasingly tied to global trade networks.

The British played a key role in facilitating Omani trade by providing protection from piracy and helping to secure Omani shipping lanes in the Persian Gulf and Indian Ocean. In return, Oman was able to export goods like frankincense, dates, and textiles, which were in high demand in Europe and Asia.

The British also introduced new technologies and infrastructure improvements, particularly in the form of port and road construction. They helped modernize Oman's transportation and communication networks, which were critical to maintaining control over the Sultanate's dispersed territories. While Oman maintained its distinct cultural and political identity, British influence was essential in shaping the country's economic modernization.

However, British influence in Oman's economy was not without its downsides. British colonial interests often led to the prioritization of British needs over those of the Omani people. For example, British traders and merchants enjoyed favorable treatment, while the local population sometimes faced economic hardships as a result of British control over key industries.

Sultan Qaboos: The Beginning of Modern Oman

By the end of the 19th century, Oman was beginning to show the signs of modernity, but it was still grappling with the legacies of its past, including its internal divisions, external influences, and reliance on trade. The stage was set for a new chapter in Oman's history, one that would be defined by the rule of Sultan Qaboos bin Said, whose leadership would bring about sweeping reforms and modernization in the country.

Sultan Qaboos ascended to the throne in 1970, and his rule would mark the beginning of a new era for Oman—one of unprecedented development, modernization, and international integration. He would work to modernize Oman's infrastructure, economy, and social systems, moving away from the traditional tribal and imamate structures toward a centralized, more progressive state.

Conclusion: Oman's Path to Modernization

The 19th century was a period of profound change for Oman. It was a time of shifting political dynamics, economic change, and growing British influence. Despite the challenges Oman faced during this period—internal division, external pressures, and the decline of its maritime empire—the Al Bu Sa'id dynasty maintained a sense of stability that allowed Oman to enter the 20th century with the foundations for modernization.

While Oman's sovereignty was increasingly challenged by British imperial interests, the country's leadership, both in Muscat and Zanzibar, was able to maintain a degree of independence that would prove crucial in the years to come. By the time Sultan Qaboos assumed power in 1970, Oman was ready for a new era of modernization, though it would carry forward the legacies of the 19th century into the contemporary world.

A BRIEF HISTORY OF OMAN

REIGN OF SULTAN QABOOS BIN SAID

The reign of Sultan Qaboos bin Said (1970-2020) represents one of the most significant and transformative periods in Oman's history. Ascending to the throne after a palace coup that ousted his father, Sultan Said bin Taimur, Sultan Qaboos became the architect of a new Oman. His vision for the country involved transforming Oman from an isolated, underdeveloped nation into a modern, stable, and prosperous state, while maintaining its unique cultural and political identity. This chapter explores the political, social, and economic changes that took place under Sultan Qaboos' rule and examines how his leadership shaped Oman's development and international standing.

The Palace Coup: Sultan Qaboos Ascends to the Throne

Sultan Qaboos bin Said ascended to the throne in 1970, following the deposition of his father, Sultan Said bin Taimur, in a palace coup. Sultan Said bin Taimur, who had ruled Oman since 1932, had implemented a conservative, isolationist policy that kept the country largely closed off from the outside world. Under his rule, Oman was mired in poverty, and its infrastructure remained underdeveloped. The country had limited access to modern education, healthcare, and economic opportunities, and the imamate system, which had long been influential in the interior, was suppressed.

Sultan Qaboos, the son of Sultan Said bin Taimur, was educated in the West, including in Britain and the United States. His exposure to modern ideas and global politics gave him a unique perspective on how Oman could be transformed. Qaboos' rise to power was precipitated by growing dissatisfaction with his father's autocratic rule, and with the help of the British government, Qaboos was able to seize power without significant bloodshed.

The new Sultan's immediate priority was to modernize Oman and address the pressing issues of poverty, lack of infrastructure, and internal conflict. To do so, he sought to establish a more inclusive, progressive, and stable government, while maintaining Oman's independence and preserving its distinct culture.

Political Reforms: Building a Modern State

One of Sultan Qaboos' first priorities was to centralize power and establish a modern political system. His reign was marked by the consolidation of authority in the hands of the Sultan, although he was careful to balance his power with consultation and careful diplomacy. Sultan Qaboos moved away from the traditional tribal and imamate structures that had characterized Oman for centuries, opting instead for a more centralized governance model.

Qaboos introduced a system that combined elements of monarchy with modern institutions, ensuring that Oman's political landscape was both stable and adaptable. While he was the head of state, Qaboos worked to implement gradual political reforms, which included the establishment of the Oman Consultative Council (Shura) in 1991. The Council was an advisory body, representing a step toward greater political participation, though real political power remained with the Sultan.

Sultan Qaboos also worked to reduce the power of the tribal factions that had historically held sway over the country. He recognized the importance of tribal loyalty, but he was determined to create a more inclusive political system that would prevent any one group from holding too much influence. This was essential for maintaining unity in a diverse nation that included various tribal, religious, and regional groups.

The Sultan was a strong believer in the importance of stability and unity, and he avoided the widespread political instability that affected many neighboring countries in the Middle East. His careful balancing of power, along with his ability to maintain Oman's independence in the face of external pressures, allowed Oman to remain largely free of the kind of authoritarianism, coups, and violent uprisings that plagued many of its neighbors.

Economic Transformation: From Poverty to Prosperity

When Sultan Qaboos came to power, Oman was a country in dire economic straits. The nation's economy was largely dependent on agriculture and traditional industries, and it had little in the way of modern infrastructure. However, Qaboos recognized that Oman's oil reserves, discovered in the 1960s, could be a key resource for the country's modernization. By the 1970s, oil had become the backbone of the Omani economy, and Qaboos moved quickly to develop the sector and use its revenues to fuel economic development.

Under his leadership, Oman invested heavily in infrastructure projects, including the construction of roads, ports, and airports, which connected the country and integrated it into the global economy. The country's ports, such as the deep-water port of Duqm, became essential for trade in the region. Oman's infrastructure improvements were also aimed at boosting tourism, which would later become an important part of the economy.

Sultan Qaboos also made significant strides in the education and healthcare sectors. He prioritized universal education, with a focus on building schools and providing opportunities for Omani youth to receive modern, secular education. This led to a generation of Omanis with the skills necessary to contribute to the country's development. Similarly, Qaboos placed a strong emphasis on healthcare, improving access to medical services throughout the country and significantly reducing infant mortality and increasing life expectancy.

By the early 21st century, Oman had transformed from a poor, isolated country into a nation with a modern infrastructure and a growing middle class. Oman's reliance on oil revenues was still significant, but the government worked to diversify the economy through investment in industries such as tourism, agriculture, manufacturing, and information technology.

A BRIEF HISTORY OF OMAN

Social Reforms: Women's Rights and National Identity

Sultan Qaboos' modernization efforts extended beyond infrastructure and economic development; he also focused on social reforms, particularly regarding women's rights and the creation of a strong national identity. Qaboos sought to move Oman away from the conservative, patriarchal norms that had been prevalent under his father's rule.

Sultan Qaboos encouraged women to participate more fully in public life. Under his rule, women gained the right to work in government and other sectors, and Qaboos pushed for greater access to education for girls. He also implemented social reforms that helped improve women's access to healthcare and other essential services. As a result, Oman became one of the more progressive countries in the Gulf in terms of women's rights, although the pace of change was gradual.

Qaboos was also deeply committed to preserving Oman's distinct cultural identity, which had been threatened by both internal divisions and external influences. He emphasized Oman's history as a seafaring nation with a rich cultural heritage, and he worked to foster a sense of national unity by promoting Omani traditions and values. Sultan Qaboos carefully balanced modernization with the preservation of Oman's unique cultural identity, and this approach earned him widespread respect from the Omani people.

Foreign Policy: A Policy of Neutrality and Diplomacy

Sultan Qaboos was an adept diplomat, and his foreign policy was defined by a pragmatic approach of neutrality, balancing

A BRIEF HISTORY OF OMAN

Oman's relations with both regional and global powers. Unlike many of his neighbors, Sultan Qaboos refrained from becoming entangled in the regional conflicts that characterized the Gulf, particularly the Iran-Iraq War (1980-1988), the Gulf War (1990-1991), and the ongoing tensions between Sunni and Shia powers in the region.

Qaboos pursued an independent foreign policy, positioning Oman as a neutral player in regional politics. Oman maintained good relations with both the West, including the United States and Britain, as well as with neighboring Gulf states, Iran, and even Yemen. Qaboos was particularly successful in maintaining cordial relations with Iran, despite the broader tension in the region. Oman's role as an intermediary in diplomacy and peace-building was further solidified in the 21st century, particularly with its mediation efforts in the nuclear negotiations between Iran and the West.

Sultan Qaboos' foreign policy helped Oman maintain its sovereignty and avoid the conflicts that plagued other Gulf states. Oman's neutral stance and diplomatic engagement made it an important player in regional and global affairs, despite its small size.

Succession and the Future of Oman

Sultan Qaboos' long reign ended with his death in January 2020, after a prolonged battle with cancer. His passing marked the end of an era for Oman, and questions about succession became a key issue for the country's future. Sultan Qaboos had no direct heirs, and his death led to the invocation of a succession plan that he had carefully laid out before his passing. The new

A BRIEF HISTORY OF OMAN

Sultan, Haitham bin Tariq Al Said, was named his successor.

Sultan Qaboos left behind a legacy of transformation and modernization, and his policies continue to shape Oman's path forward. Under his leadership, Oman became a modern, stable, and prosperous nation, and his foreign policy of neutrality and diplomacy has given the country an influential role in global politics.

Conclusion: The Enduring Legacy of Sultan Qaboos

The reign of Sultan Qaboos bin Said was one of the most transformative periods in Oman's history. His vision of a modern, stable, and prosperous Oman was realized through his policies of economic development, social reform, and diplomatic engagement. Qaboos' ability to balance modernization with the preservation of Oman's unique culture and traditions has left a lasting legacy that will continue to shape the country in the years to come.

As Oman enters the post-Qaboos era, the challenge for the new leadership will be to continue his legacy while navigating the complexities of a rapidly changing world. Sultan Qaboos' reign stands as a testament to the power of visionary leadership and the transformative potential of a country committed to progress while staying true to its heritage.

CONCLUSION

Oman's history is a testament to the resilience, adaptability, and vision of its people. From its ancient maritime roots, when it controlled vast trade networks across the Arabian Sea, to its present-day status as a modern, stable, and prosperous nation, Oman has navigated centuries of political upheavals, economic challenges, and cultural transformations. This brief history of Oman reveals not only the country's remarkable journey but also the enduring values that have shaped its identity: independence, hospitality, peace, and a commitment to progress without losing sight of its heritage.

Throughout its history, Oman has been a place of convergence—a crossroads where East meets West, where diverse cultures and religions have blended over the centuries. The Omani people have always been guided by a sense of unity and pride in their unique culture, and this has allowed them to weather the many storms that have marked their past.

From the early days of the ancient civilizations in Oman,

through the rise and fall of various dynasties, to the colonial influences of the British and the visionary leadership of Sultan Qaboos bin Said, Oman's journey has been one of transformation and renewal. Each era, with its own set of challenges, has left its mark on the country, but Oman's ability to adapt and evolve has been a constant.

A Legacy of Leadership: The Vision of Sultan Qaboos

At the heart of modern Oman's transformation stands Sultan Qaboos bin Said, whose leadership from 1970 to 2020 guided the country through an unprecedented period of change. His vision for Oman was one of modernization—transforming a nation from one that had been isolated and underdeveloped into one that is globally integrated, economically viable, and socially progressive. The Sultan's legacy is not only seen in the country's physical infrastructure, which has seen remarkable growth in roads, ports, and cities, but also in its social landscape, with greater opportunities for education, healthcare, and women's participation in public life.

Under Sultan Qaboos, Oman pursued a path of neutrality and diplomacy that allowed the country to maintain peace and stability in a region often marred by conflict. The Sultan's ability to navigate Oman through the complexities of Middle Eastern politics, while preserving its independence and fostering cooperation with both regional and global powers, has left an indelible mark on the country's foreign policy.

But beyond tangible accomplishments, Sultan Qaboos' true legacy lies in the values he instilled in Oman—a commitment to development rooted in respect for tradition, a culture of moderation, and a deep sense of pride in Oman's identity. This delicate balance of modernity and tradition is what continues to define Oman as it moves forward into the 21st century.

Oman's Path Forward: Challenges and Opportunities

As Oman enters the post-Qaboos era, the path forward will require maintaining the same spirit of resilience and vision that has characterized the country throughout its history. The passing of Sultan Qaboos created a void that has raised questions about the future, but the country's stable political system and the succession plan that was put in place reassure many that the transition to new leadership will be smooth. Sultan Haitham bin Tariq, the new Sultan, inherits a country poised for continued progress.

The challenges Oman faces in the future are not insignificant. Like many countries in the Gulf, Oman's economy remains heavily dependent on oil, and the world's transition to more sustainable energy sources presents both an opportunity and a challenge. Diversifying the economy, enhancing the private sector, and creating new industries—particularly in tourism, technology, and education—will be crucial for sustaining Oman's prosperity in the coming decades.

Oman must also navigate the complexities of a rapidly changing geopolitical landscape. While the country has built a reputation for neutrality and diplomacy, tensions in the wider Middle East—especially in the Gulf—could affect Oman's ability to maintain its independent stance. Ensuring continued peace and stability will require skillful leadership and a commitment to dialogue and cooperation.

Furthermore, the younger generations of Omanis, who have benefited from the educational reforms initiated by Sultan Qaboos, will likely play an increasingly prominent role in shaping the country's future. Harnessing their energy, creativity, and innovative potential will be key to ensuring that Oman remains on the cutting edge of global developments.

Oman's Unique Identity in a Globalized World

One of the key factors in Oman's success has been its ability to retain its unique cultural identity, despite the pressures of modernization and globalization. Oman has always been a proud nation, one that values its history, traditions, and connection to the wider world. Its ancient heritage, combined with its modern achievements, provides a solid foundation upon which to build the future.

As Oman continues to evolve, it will face the challenge of balancing its cultural traditions with the demands of an increasingly interconnected world. The preservation of its distinctive cultural practices, its architectural heritage, and its linguistic and religious diversity will be essential in maintaining the sense of identity that has made Oman a beacon of stability and moderation in the Gulf region.

Oman's vision for the future is rooted in a commitment to development, both economically and socially, while remaining grounded in the values that have defined its people for millennia. As it navigates the complexities of the 21st century, Oman will continue to be a model of progress, moderation, and resilience in an increasingly globalized world.

A BRIEF HISTORY OF OMAN

A Future of Promise

Oman's journey through history has been marked by remarkable achievements and challenges, but through it all, the country has remained true to its values of independence, peace, and progress. From the ancient seafaring civilizations to the modern state that Sultan Qaboos helped build, Oman has demonstrated the power of vision, leadership, and a deep connection to its heritage.

As the nation enters a new chapter, the spirit of resilience and the commitment to modernization without compromising tradition will remain central to its future. Oman's role in the Gulf and the wider world will continue to grow as it adapts to new global realities, building upon the foundation laid by its forebears and by Sultan Qaboos' transformative leadership.

Oman's story is one of evolution—a narrative of a country that has overcome adversity, embraced change, and charted its own course in a world of uncertainty. As the sun sets on the era of Sultan Qaboos, the future of Oman remains bright, and its people will undoubtedly continue to carry forward the legacy of a nation that has always sought to build bridges rather than walls, to seek peace rather than conflict, and to embrace progress while remaining true to its roots.

This is the story of Oman—a country with a rich history, a promising future, and an enduring commitment to the values that have defined it for centuries.

APPENDIX

Key Historical Events

- The Arrival of Islam (7th Century): The introduction of Islam to Oman is a turning point in its history. Islam spread through the region, influencing both the religious and political structure of Oman. The Omanis embraced the Ibadi sect of Islam, which continues to shape the country's religious practices and identity to this day.

- The Rise of the Omani Imamate (8th Century): The imamate system, where religious leaders also served as political rulers, played a pivotal role in Oman's governance for centuries. This system fostered a unique balance between religious and political authority, which remains an integral part of Omani identity.

- The Portuguese Occupation (1507–1650): The Portuguese seized control of key Omani ports in the early 16th century, including Muscat and other coastal towns. The Portuguese occupation disrupted Oman's maritime trade routes, but it also set the stage for the eventual resurgence of Omani power in the region.

- The Expulsion of the Portuguese and the Rise of the Al Ya'rubi Dynasty (1650): In 1650, Oman successfully ousted the Portuguese from its ports, beginning a period of renewed strength and territorial expansion. The Al Ya'rubi dynasty, which took control during this time, played a crucial role in Oman's rise as a regional maritime power.

- The Omani Empire (18th Century): During the 18th century, Oman established itself as a dominant power in the Indian Ocean, with control over parts of East Africa, Persia, and the Arabian Peninsula. The empire thrived on trade and its strategic location between Africa, Asia, and the Arabian Gulf.

- The Al Bu Said Dynasty and the Founding of Modern Oman (1749): The Al Bu Said dynasty, which remains in power today, was founded in 1749 when Ahmad bin Said became the Sultan of Oman. His descendants have ruled Oman continuously, overseeing periods of both prosperity and struggle.

- The British Influence (19th Century): In the 19th century, Oman entered into a series of treaties with the British, culminating in British influence over Oman's foreign policy. The British served as key advisers, although Oman remained nominally independent.

- The Dhofar Rebellion (1962–1975): A major conflict in southern Oman, the Dhofar Rebellion was a Marxist-led insurgency against the Sultan's government. The rebellion, with support from neighboring countries like South Yemen and the

A BRIEF HISTORY OF OMAN

Soviet Union, lasted for over a decade. Sultan Qaboos bin Said, upon ascending to the throne, successfully quelled the insurgency with military and political reforms.

- The Accession of Sultan Qaboos bin Said (1970): Sultan Qaboos bin Said deposed his father, Sultan Said bin Taimur, in a palace coup in 1970. This marked the beginning of a new era for Oman, characterized by modernization, development, and the opening up of the country to the world.

- Oman's Modernization and Development (1970-2020): Under Sultan Qaboos, Oman underwent significant political, economic, and social reforms. The country modernized its infrastructure, expanded education and healthcare, and developed a more inclusive political system, while maintaining its unique cultural heritage.

- The Death of Sultan Qaboos bin Said (2020): Sultan Qaboos passed away in January 2020 after a prolonged battle with cancer. His death marked the end of an era of leadership that had shaped Oman for nearly five decades. The succession plan was smoothly carried out, with Sultan Haitham bin Tariq becoming the new ruler.

Key Figures

- Sultan Said bin Taimur (1910-1972): The father of Sultan Qaboos, Sultan Said bin Taimur ruled Oman with a conservative, isolationist approach. His reign was marked by stagnation and internal unrest, particularly in the interior regions, which led to his eventual overthrow.

A BRIEF HISTORY OF OMAN

- Sultan Qaboos bin Said (1940-2020): The longest-reigning monarch in Omani history, Sultan Qaboos is credited with transforming Oman from a backwater, isolated state into a modern, prosperous nation. His leadership was defined by modernization, diplomacy, and the pursuit of peaceful relations in a volatile region.

- Imam Ahmad bin Said (1738-1783): The first ruler of the Al Bu Said dynasty, Imam Ahmad bin Said was instrumental in establishing the Al Bu Said family's dominance in Oman. His leadership laid the foundation for the Omani Empire's expansion in the 18th century.

- Imam Azzan bin Qais (1624-1679): A prominent figure during the rise of the Al Ya'rubi dynasty, Imam Azzan bin Qais was key in the expulsion of the Portuguese from Oman's coastal regions, marking the beginning of Oman's resurgence as a maritime power.

- Sultan Haitham bin Tariq (1954–Present): The current Sultan of Oman, Haitham bin Tariq succeeded Sultan Qaboos in 2020. Haitham, a cousin of Qaboos, has worked to continue his predecessor's policies of modernization while exploring new paths to diversify Oman's economy and maintain its role as a diplomatic player in the Gulf.

Key Terms and Concepts

- Ibadi Islam: A sect of Islam practiced by the majority of Omanis, distinguishing them from the Sunni and Shia branches. Ibadi Islam is known for its emphasis on community consultation and moderation.

A BRIEF HISTORY OF OMAN

- The Imamate System: A political and religious structure where the Imam, a religious leader, also served as the political leader of Oman. The system existed for centuries but was ultimately replaced by the Sultanate after the rise of the Al Bu Said dynasty.

- Dhofar Rebellion (1962-1975): An insurgency in southern Oman led by Marxist groups against the ruling Sultanate. It was largely supported by South Yemen and other communist allies. The rebellion ended after extensive military campaigns led by Sultan Qaboos.

- The Al Bu Said Dynasty: The ruling family of Oman since 1749. The dynasty has overseen Oman's rise as a regional maritime power and its transition into a modern state under Sultan Qaboos.

- Oman's Neutral Foreign Policy: Oman's approach to international relations, characterized by neutrality and diplomatic engagement rather than alignment with any particular regional or global power. This policy has allowed Oman to act as a mediator in regional disputes and maintain peaceful relations with both the Gulf States and non-Gulf powers.

- The 1970 Palace Coup: The event that led to Sultan Qaboos bin Said assuming the throne, following the ousting of his father, Sultan Said bin Taimur. The coup marked the beginning of Oman's modernization process.

- The Sultan's Vision for Development: Sultan Qaboos' broad agenda for modernizing Oman's economy, education, healthcare, and infrastructure, which helped transform the country into one of the wealthiest and most developed nations in the region by the 21st century.

ABOUT THE AUTHOR

KJ Smith is an amateur historian with a passion for exploring the diverse cultures and histories of the world. With a keen interest in uncovering the stories that shape nations, KJ brings a unique perspective to the *A Brief History Of - Around the World Edition* series, offering readers a concise yet insightful look into the history of each country. When not writing, KJ enjoys traveling and further deepening their knowledge of global history.

Printed in Dunstable, United Kingdom